SPEKE HALL

Merseyside

THE NATIONAL TRUST

Speke is on the north bank of the Mersey, 1 mile off the A561 on the west side of Liverpool airport.

Speke has been much studied and written about, and I have drawn greatly on the work of others in compiling this guidebook. In particular I would like to thank Tony Tibbles, writer of the previous guidebook and now Curator at the Merseyside Maritime Museum, for his continuing interest and help. In addition, Dr Jennifer Lewis, assisted by her colleagues in the Archaeology Department of Liverpool University, has undertaken surveys at Speke Hall whenever building work has offered opportunities for closer inspection, and the resulting meticulous reports have greatly added to our knowledge of the building, for which the Trust is most grateful. Assistance in garnering information has also been received from many others; the help of Roy Boardman, Custodian at Speke, and Peter Denlow, who has researched the Watt family, is here acknowledged with particular gratitude.

Belinda Cousens

Photographs: Bridgeman Art Library p.38; Conway Library, Courtauld Institute of Art p.40; Hunterian Museum & Art Gallery, University of Glasgow p.43; Liverpool Record Office (Binns Collection) p.37 (below); National Museums, Liverpool pp.33, 35; National Trust Photographic Library p.45; NTPL/Andreas von Einsiedel pp.12, 16; NTPL/Geoffrey Frosh pp.5, 8, 10, 14, 18, 21, 22, 36, 39, 42; NTPL/John Hammond pp.4, 11, 15, 17, 19, 26, 31, 41, 44, back cover; NTPL/Rupert Truman front cover, pp.1, 7, 24, 25, 27, 28, 32, 37 (above); Norwyn Ltd p.29.

First published in Great Britain in 1994 by the National Trust
© 1994 The National Trust
Registered charity no. 205846
Reprinted 1996, 1999, 2001; revised 2003, 2006, 2009

ISBN 978-1-84359-089-7

Designed by James Shurmer

Phototypeset in Monotype Bembo Series 270
by Intraspan Ltd, Smallfield, Surrey (SG2043)

Printed by Hawthornes
for National Trust (Enterprises) Ltd, Heelis, Kemble Drive,
Swindon, Wilts SN2 2NA
on stock made from 75% recycled fibre

CONTENTS

Introduction   *page* 5

Plans of the House   6

Chapter One Tour of the House   7

Chapter Two History of the Building   23

Chapter Three The Garden   29

Chapter Four The Estate   33

Chapter Five The Owners of Speke   35

Family Tree of the Norrises and Beauclerks   46

Family Tree of the Watts   47

Bibliography   48

INTRODUCTION

The approach to Speke Hall, through the industrial suburbs of twentieth-century Liverpool, serves only to enhance the outstanding rarity and romance of this remarkable building. Speke is one of the four most important surviving timber-framed buildings in the north of England. The extensive Victorian recreation of its interiors in the antiquarian spirit has only increased its value and interest.

Built by the Norris family in stages during the sixteenth century, Speke reached its present form in 1598, the date firmly recorded by Edward Norris over the main entrance. When it passed by marriage to the Beauclerk family in the eighteenth century, it entered into a period of neglect and even dereliction.

When in 1795 Speke was sold, for the only time in its 500-year history, it was acquired by a wealthy local merchant, Richard Watt, who had made his fortune in the West Indies. He thus became the owner of a derelict house, entirely devoid of contents, but which may already have acquired a value as a romantic survivor from the Elizabethan era. A partial restoration took place in the early 1800s, but it was not until the mid-nineteenth century that a full restoration was carried out by Richard Watt V. It is this refurbishment of the 1850s that now provides the chief character of the interiors, which were enhanced by the additions of Frederick Leyland in the Arts and Crafts taste a decade later.

The last owner of Speke was Adelaide Watt, Richard Watt's orphaned daughter. She never married and devoted her life to preserving Speke Hall and enhancing its estate. When she died in 1921, in a remarkable act of historical piety she left Speke to trustees of the original Norris family who had built the house. However, anticipating that the expansion of Liverpool might make the property less attractive as a domestic dwelling, she included a secondary clause bequeathing Speke to the National Trust. This finally came about in 1943, and Speke was leased first to Liverpool City Council and later to the National Museums, Liverpoool, which undertook a major programme of repairs to the building, grant-aided by the Historic Buildings and Monuments Commission. In 1986 the National Trust took over direct management, supported by an annual grant from the National Museums and Galleries on Merseyside, and further restoration work is continuing, particularly on the contents and in the grounds.

(Left) The north entrance; coloured lithograph by Joseph Nash, 1849 (Tapestry Bedroom)

(Right) The Green Bedroom. The decoration reflects Richard Watt V's refurbishment of Speke in the 1850s

PLANS OF THE HOUSE

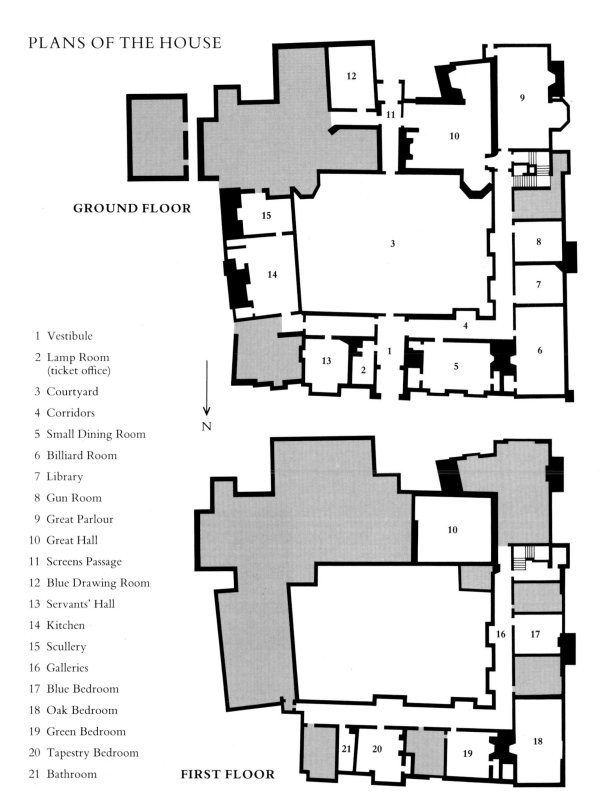

GROUND FLOOR

N

1 Vestibule

2 Lamp Room
   (ticket office)

3 Courtyard

4 Corridors

5 Small Dining Room

6 Billiard Room

7 Library

8 Gun Room

9 Great Parlour

10 Great Hall

11 Screens Passage

12 Blue Drawing Room

13 Servants' Hall

14 Kitchen

15 Scullery

16 Galleries

17 Blue Bedroom

18 Oak Bedroom

19 Green Bedroom

20 Tapestry Bedroom

21 Bathroom

FIRST FLOOR

CHAPTER ONE

TOUR OF THE HOUSE

THE COURTYARD

The impression of symmetry created by this courtyard is a misleading one, since it was built in several phases over at least two centuries. The oldest part of the present building, a cruck-beamed hall of the fourteenth century, lies concealed in the south-east section, behind the compass bay on the left. This bay was added much later, probably to balance that on the right, both of them flanking and lending prominence to the pilastered doorway in the centre. This was the original front door, leading into the Screens Passage and the Great Hall. In Tudor times, and indeed until the nineteenth-century alterations, visitors would have crossed the Moat Bridge and

passed through the gatehouse and across the courtyard to this entrance.

Above the entrance door, in the eaves, is a small hole, enabling the occupant of a concealed space behind to spy on those arriving – a rare example of the original 'eavesdrop' and particularly useful for a Catholic family like the Norrises.

The present Great Hall of *c*.1530, which completed the south range, was built by William Norris II. Shortly afterwards he added the parlour block in the south-west corner, and, lastly, the west range in the 1550s. The pattern established by him, of diagonal bracing to the timber frame, which is set on a sandstone plinth, is repeated on all four sides, along with the quatrefoils in the panels between the two floors. The main posts display an unusual scroll motif, which is cut out of the solid timber and also

(Below)   The north end of the Courtyard

contributes to the consistent rhythm of the four elevations. The main façade of the Great Hall in particular displays the original carpenter's numbering system on the timbers, to ensure that they were correctly put together on site.

Edward Norris inherited Speke from his father in 1568. He continued with the rebuilding, adding the east range in stages and finally, in 1598, he completed the courtyard with the north range, as confirmed by the inscription on the gatehouse. In the north-east corner, there are four panels of bracing in a pattern entirely unknown elsewhere.

The courtyard is dominated by two magnificent yews, traditionally known as Adam and Eve. Their age is uncertain but the first mention of them occurs in 1712, when Ezekial Mason was paid for 'making Frames to set about ye yew trees in the Court'. The sandstone piscina may come from Childwall church, which was partially rebuilt in 1833. Until the 1940s, only the central path was cobbled.

The fireplace in the Small Dining Room

THE SMALL DINING ROOM

The decorations in this, and the following three rooms and the adjoining passage, are all the product of Frederick Leyland's completion of the restoration of Speke, which he leased in 1867. His family found the Great Hall, which had been re-furnished by Richard Watt V in baronial style, draughty and inconvenient, so this Dining Room was created out of two smaller rooms. The panelling is entirely of this date.

FIREPLACE

The sandstone fire surround was copied for Leyland from an early seventeenth-century fireplace then surviving in the ruins of the Old Hutt at nearby Halewood. This relic had been noted by Matthew Gregson in 1820, and was also copied by Leyland in two other rooms.

The blue-and-white tiles to the fireplace cheeks are in the style of William de Morgan, but are slightly inferior to his usual standard and may be Dutch imports, as his designs were quickly imitated by others. The overmantel, which also forms part of the 1860s scheme, is made up of Dutch tiles showing a view of Elsenburg, a house near Utrecht, based on an engraving of 1719.

PICTURES

In Miss Watt's time, this became her Morning Room where she also conducted business with her tenants. Her portrait, a lithograph taken to mark her coming of age in 1878, hangs to the right of the fireplace. Underneath it is a copy of a silhouette of her ancestor, Richard Watt I (1724–96).

Apart from the portraits the pictures here are all nineteenth-century views of Speke Hall. The large watercolour by W. G. Herdman dated 1860 shows the west corner of the moat shortly after it had been turned into a formal garden and replanted by Richard Watt V. The coloured lithographs by Nash and Dodd, all of the 1840s, show romantic interpretations of Speke.

FURNITURE

The pair of mahogany cane-seated armchairs of c.1800 are stamped STARKIE, and must have belonged to Miss Watt's relations, the Starkies of Ashton Hall in Lancashire, with whom she frequently stayed. Of the same date is the handsome mahogany longcase clock by J. & P. Hendrick of Liverpool, the case displaying a curious mixture of Egyptian and Gothic motifs. The seventeenth-century-style high-back chairs upholstered in red leather are part of Richard Watt V's re-furnishing at

Speke. The eighteenth-century Dutch marquetry cabinet also represents popular mid-Victorian taste.

CERAMICS

On the sideboard and dining table are various pieces from two dinner services used by Miss Watt, the blue-and-white transfer-printed set by Copeland, and a plain white with blue border bearing a Watt arms and crest. The latter service had been sold after her father's death, but was bought back by Miss Watt in 1880.

In the cabinet are two patterns of Chinese porcelain dinner services in *famille rose*, made for the European market in the eighteenth century.

THE CORRIDORS

The design of the Elizabethan Speke is unusual in having passages on two sides of the courtyard. The more common plan at this date, as found at Little Moreton Hall in Cheshire for instance, was for rooms to interlink. The Speke arrangement gives a greater degree of privacy, and is reminiscent of the monastic plan.

The present appearance of the corridors is entirely due to Frederick Leyland, who installed the dark stained panelling to dado height, the doors with decorated lintels copied from those of the Screens Passage, and shelves over to display his blue-and-white china. The wallpaper also represents his taste, although renewed in the 1940s. Called 'Trellis', it is one of the earliest wallpaper designs by William Morris, first printed in 1864.

FURNITURE

The furniture along these corridors was mostly purchased by Richard Watt V. The pair of massive X-frame armchairs was intended to furnish the Great Hall, their ornate backs formed of seventeenth-century continental carvings of biblical scenes. The carved brackets on the window wall were for oil lamps, electric lighting not being installed at Speke until the 1930s.

THE BILLIARD ROOM

This is the first room in the west range, which was added *c.*1550. In the mid-nineteenth century this part of the house was described as 'a complete wreck' and it remained so until Leyland undertook the final phase of restoration at Speke in 1867. This room had previously been a kitchen.

Excavations which took place here during recent building repairs identified a watercourse and some 1½ yards of infill underneath the present floor level. Analysis of the various materials has thrown light on the lifestyle of the early Norrises in medieval times, before the building of this range in the mid-sixteenth century. Pottery included whiteware and stoneware imported from the Continent. Bones revealed a diet which may have included dogs as well as the more usual domestic animals and a wide variety of birds.

Leyland's restoration included a new stone-flagged floor and probably complete reglazing of the windows.

FIREPLACE

The sandstone fireplace installed by Leyland is identical to that in the Small Dining Room and the Oak Bedroom. Here the tiles are a Pugin design manufactured by Mintons.

PICTURES

The plain decorations were no doubt intended as a foil to the pictures Leyland would have hung here. By this date he had already established a considerable collection of Pre-Raphaelites as well as Old Masters, including works by Rembrandt and Velázquez (see p.43).

In Miss Watt's time the walls were hung with portraits of Richard Watt III's racehorses by Ferneley, Marshall and Herring Senior, and the room was used as a dining-room. Today a portrait of Frederick Leyland, on loan from the Walker Art Gallery, is flanked by engravings: one, in colour, of Colonel W. Hall Walker by Lynwood Palmer, 1910; and another of St Agnes Church, Liverpool, by W. V. Collett, dated 1904. The elegant sailing boat, painted by De Simone in two pictures dated 1864, is the *Diadem*, one of several yachts owned by Richard Watt V. The animal paintings include works by Clifton Tomson and E. B. Chalon.

FURNITURE

The billiard table by Thurstons is on loan from Dunham Massey in Cheshire, Miss Watt having presented her father's to the local men's club. The carpet-covered chairs are typical Victorian pieces, which have survived in remarkable condition. No designer is known for the three Gothic side-tables, the nearest of which carries a glazed case containing an illuminated address presented to Miss Watt by the tenants of the estate on her coming of age. The silver-plated reading lamp was probably bought from Mappin & Webb by Miss Watt, who did much of her shopping by mail order.

THE LIBRARY

Previously a scullery, this room too is entirely the result of Leyland's restoration, including the false timber posts dividing the walls. The wallpaper is 'Pomegranate', another of William Morris's early designs, printed in 1864. Behind the bookshelves is his pattern 'Daisy' on a green ground.

FIREPLACE

The etiolated columns framing the fireplace are modelled on those in the Great Hall and the tiles set into the cast-iron grate are Liverpool pottery.

The Library

FURNITURE

The pair of rush-seated 'Sussex' chairs must also have been introduced by Leyland and were probably supplied by Morris & Co.

BOOKS AND PICTURES

The books mostly belonged to Miss Watt and illustrate her interest in estate matters and agricultural practice as well as the more predictable feminine reading such as religious topics and novels. The pictures all belonged to Miss Watt and include lithographs of Tatton Sykes, a neighbour of the Watts in Yorkshire, hanging alongside the portrait of Napoleon after Baron Gros. An illuminated address from the parishioners of Garston church to commemorate her coming of age, signed by her uncle Hewson, hangs on the right.

THE GUN ROOM

This may be the 'ould chappell' mentioned in the 1624 inventory, by which time it was being used as a storeroom. It is now decorated in a very similar manner to the Library, except here the 'Daisy' pattern on a white ground is used. This paper has been severely stained by pollution, and has recently been cleaned.

This room was much used in the 1920s and '30s when Speke was in the hands of trustees and only infrequently lived in. During the shooting season the house would briefly come to life with regular shooting parties on two Saturdays a month. As we have not inherited the guns, racks and associated furniture relating to its function as a gun room, this room will be used to display temporary exhibitions relating to the history of Speke Hall and the families who have lived here.

THE GREAT HALL

As with most Tudor houses, tradition and imagination have played their part in creating the story of Speke, and nowhere more so than in the Great Hall. Even now, with the benefits of scientific and archaeological analysis, much remains conjectural. Science has, however, established a firm period for the building. Dendrochronology, by which the

The Great Hall; one of Joseph Nash's romantic watercolours of Speke, painted in 1849

rings in the timber are compared with known dated examples, has revealed that some of the major structural timber was felled in 1530. This is later than previously thought, and means that this splendid hall was built by Sir William Norris II, who inherited Speke in 1524 at the age of 23. By this time a Great Hall of this scale would have been a status symbol, but no longer used as the main eating room.

The original appearance of the Hall would have been dictated by the five vast timber posts on each length, now just visible above the panelling, their moulding conforming with that of the ceiling timbers. The walls may originally have been hung with tapestries.

In Leyland's time, the panelling must have been obscured by the paintings he hung here, which included a Velázquez and Whistler's full-length portraits of his mother and of Frederick Leyland. The Leylands adopted the lifestyle of the lord of the manor and are recorded in 1869 as entertaining some 80 children from the estate to a full Christmas meal and parlour games. In Miss Watt's time tenants' dinners took place here.

WAINSCOT

An inscription now lost recorded that Sir William installed the wainscot in 1564. In fact, there are several different patterns of panelling here, suggesting adaptation over the centuries. The decorated panels comprising carved busts framed by slender columns, traditionally said to have been looted from the Palace of Holyrood in Edinburgh by Sir William, are more likely to have been installed by his son Edward. His arms appear on the timber porch framing the west doorway, along with those of his wife, Margaret Smallwood. Her family were merchants in the Low Countries, which is a more likely source for this style of carving of *c.*1570.

BAY WINDOWS

Originally, the only windows in the Hall may have been the upper clerestory. However, the bay window facing on to the courtyard must have been

The 'Great Wainscot', which was installed in the Great Hall by Sir William Norris in 1564

added shortly after, as its construction preceded the west range of *c*.1550. The bay to the south is more puzzling. Although the fireplace is not at right-angles to the Hall, the external decoration of the sandstone with a curved cove and billeting underneath corresponds exactly with the timber framing of the Hall. Possibly the base of the chimney is set on pre-existing foundations.

FIREPLACE

Most perplexing of all is the main fireplace with its vast ornamented overmantel. The fact that this cuts through the ceiling decoration and extends across a window on the north side, might suggest that the fireplace is a later addition, but there is no hint of a fireplace elsewhere in the Hall. Its position against the Screens Passage is certainly unusual but a similar plan existed at Denton Hall in east Cheshire, which also boasted a comparable overmantel.

It has been suggested that this overmantel is entirely of nineteenth-century construction, based on a drawing by George Bullock, who was restoring the room in 1808. Bullock's drawing is only fully executed and measured in the area of the fire surround, which is of red Mona marble and is undoubtedly his work; and the sketch of the overmantel is accompanied by a note recording that it was 'composed of oak and burnt red Clay'. A brick overmantel with similar motifs of crenellations and pinnacles can be found at Little Moreton Hall. Herringbone brickwork was revealed beneath the lower section of the plaster during repairs. The massive oak mantel beam, with its carved cable and vine decoration, is entirely consistent with the date of the Hall. It may only have been in the mid-nineteenth century that the overmantel was plastered over.

FLOOR

Bullock also restored the pink and white limestone paving. Identified as a Swedish limestone, of a type being imported in the seventeenth century, this may have been reused from another building.

FURNITURE

The seventeenth-century furniture now displayed here has been chosen to suggest the appearance of this room during the Norris era. In fact much of it was purchased by the Watt family, but dispersed about the house, and many pieces have restorations of this date.

The distinctive scalloped cresting to several of the panelled chairs is typical of the south Lancashire tradition. The large press cupboard, on which the best plate would have been displayed, has had an extra shelf added above.

ARMOUR

The arrangement of armour over the fireplace is based on a photograph of 1904, and the shield with its display of halberds and spontoons may well date from the 1856 refurbishment. The steel armour arranged on the mantel beam is part of an important set which may have been made at the royal workshop at Greenwich c.1630 for the Yeomen of the Guard. The full-length suit of armour standing in the north bay is Victorian, imitating Italian armour c.1580, with an electrotype helmet in the style of Henri II (1519–59).

PICTURE

The full-length portrait hanging in the north bay is of John Middleton, 'The Childe of Hale'. This young man was born in the nearby village of Hale in 1578, and was exhibited at the Court of James I on account of his great height, having reached 9ft 3in before he was twenty. The portrait (formerly at High Legh Hall) was probably painted after his death in 1623.

STAINED GLASS

Speke Hall was substantially reglazed in the nineteenth-century restorations, when the few surviving sections of decorative glass were rearranged and new pieces added, including several quarries bearing the initials 'WN' for William Norris. In the south bay are two sixteenth-century Flemish roundels of *Our Lady of Mercy* and *Adam and Eve*. In the north bay, on the right, are fragments of medieval glass said to have been brought by Miss Watt from the old church at Garston, demolished in 1876. The heraldic panels are seventeenth-century, some representing local families related to the Norrises.

THE SCREENS PASSAGE

This would have been the principal entrance to Speke Hall in the sixteenth century, and indeed remained so until the Victorian alterations. Its status is signified by the carved detailing to the door surrounds and the richly moulded and chamfered ceiling beams, which also continue in the adjoining passage. In the nineteenth century the walls were decorated with illusionistic timber framing.

THE BLUE DRAWING ROOM

This must be the Little Parlour described in the 1624 inventory, when it was furnished with upholstery, curtains and table 'carpetts', all in blue. Other items listed, including backgammon boards, a chess board and toasting forks, suggest this was a room much used by the family. By 1700, the fifteen stools had been replaced and the room contained the extraordinary number of 24 chairs, most of them upholstered in leather or tapestry.

It was unusual for a family room of this date to be set behind the Screens Passage, in the area usually reserved for the domestic offices. A late seventeenth-century bill mentions 'penting of Mr. Norrises Little Parler' and behind the wallpaper panelling of this date survives, crudely grained to represent walnut. Leyland apparently hung the walls with a grey fluted satin. The present Morris 'Willow' wallpaper, first produced in 1874, is a recent replacement of that originally hung here in 1934.

FIREPLACE

Leyland replaced the fireplace with the present marble surround and tiles in the Japanese spirit which became fashionable after the International Exhibition of 1862. The brass and iron grate is decorated with sunflowers, a leitmotif of the Arts and Crafts movement. This also appears on the oak door surround, along with the cross of the Molyneux family, showing Leyland's work at Speke again combining an antiquarian interest with the fashionable Arts and Crafts taste.

FURNITURE

The extensive suite of tulipwood and ormolu furniture in Louis XV style may have been bought at the time of the marriage of Richard Watt and Adelaide Hignett in 1856. It was probably supplied by a Liverpool furniture warehouse, but the maker is unknown for all except the piano, which is by Dreapers of Liverpool. A further settee, an ottoman

*The Blue Drawing
Room*

and an overmantel mirror have been lost from the suite, but nevertheless the room conveys precisely the claustrophobic clutter as well as the foreign style which William Morris sought to counteract. The suite provoked the derision of Leyland, who likened the room to 'a French plum box' and banished the furniture to the storeroom.

PICTURES

In 1624 a map of Jerusalem and a 'great callendar' hung on the walls. Now the pictures include several views of Speke Hall: to the left of the fireplace an oil painting of the hall from across the South Lawn, by J. Suker, 1865; immediately to the right of the doorway a large watercolour of the north gatehouse by Joseph Nash and next to it a small oil painting showing the Great Hall *c.*1860 with its baronial furnishing.

CERAMICS

The numerous ceramics here all belonged to Miss Watt. The handsome indigo blue and gilt vases are Copeland, apart from the lidded Worcester vase. The several unglazed figure groups are all by George Joult of Staffordshire.

Visitors are now asked to retrace their footsteps through the Great Hall and turn left into the Great Parlour.

THE GREAT PARLOUR

Externally, this room and that above form a separate unit, set at right-angles to the Great Hall with its roof line and height quite different from that of the adjoining west range. Nevertheless, its construction is known to have followed on shortly after the Great Hall, since its timbers were felled in the succeeding year, 1531.

The scale of the room illustrates the status and ambitions of the Norris family at this date. Whereas the Little Parlour was used for family amusements, this would have been a largely ceremonial room.

During the eighteenth century this part of the house fell into decay and this room was described in 1855 as 'a complete ruin; the [inlaid oak] floor has been entirely removed; every window is boarded up; mouldings from the wainscot are crumbling; . . . and the ivy has in many places forced itself through from the outside'. As a consequence, the lower parts of the panelling are in stained softwood rather than the original oak.

CEILING

The chief feature of the room, the ornate plaster ceiling, is a later enhancement, perhaps executed in 1612, which is the date on the sandstone porch leading to the garden. Originally the main ceiling beams, richly moulded, were left exposed in the manner of the ceiling of the Withdrawing Room at Little Moreton Hall. The plaster ceiling to the bay is of later date, and probably contemporary with the building of the bay c.1630.

FIREPLACE

The carved overmantel to the fireplace was also added later, c.1567. Sadly, Speke lacks portraits of its early creators, but here they are all represented, rather in the style of a frieze on a tomb. In the centre is Sir William Norris II, flanked by his two wives and with their nineteen children represented beneath. Even the death of his eldest son and heir, William III, who was killed at the Battle of Pinkie in 1547, seems to be represented in the prostrate naked figure at the bottom. In the left-hand panel is William II's father, Henry, with his wife Clemence and their five children, whilst to the right is his heir

The Great Parlour; coloured lithograph by Joseph Nash, 1846 (Great Parlour)

The ornate plasterwork ceiling is a later addition to the Great Parlour, perhaps put up in 1612

Edward, together with his wife Margaret and two of their nine children. In place of the additional children is a cartouche bearing the family crest, the erne (eagle), which was granted only in 1567 and may indicate the date of this touchingly primitive family record.

FURNITURE

The 1624 inventory indicates a large matching suite of furniture not dissimilar in purpose to the Victorian suite now filling the room. The earlier colour scheme was green, used for curtains, table-carpets, and upholstery for the 2 forms, 24 stools, 3 chairs and 2 little chairs. By 1700 the forms and stools had been replaced by 14 chairs, upholstered in 'setwork' or tapestry, and 8 turned chairs.

Today the room is largely furnished as it was in 1867, when it also contained a baby grand piano. The suite of chairs and settees upholstered in crimson Utrecht velvet is typical of the antiquarian style of furniture introduced by Richard Watt V. At the end of the room is the massive oak buffet originally intended for the Great Hall. It comprises numerous pieces of older carving, including at the back a Flemish panel *c.*1580. This depicts a biblical scene in which Esther pleads with her husband King Ahasuerus on behalf of her fellow Jews, an event still commemorated in the Jewish festival of Purim. The small cabinet on stand flanking the doorway also contains older carvings, including three scenes depicting Adam and Eve. This piece was supplied by Wrights of Wardour Street, one of the largest of the many dealers in London specialising in such antiquarian furniture in the mid-nineteenth century.

PICTURES

Opposite the fireplace hangs a watercolour view of this room painted in 1846 by Joseph Nash, who through his volumes *The Mansions of England in the Olden Time* probably did more than anyone to promote the fashionable Victorian enthusiasm for antiquarian interiors. Indeed it may have been precisely his images which influenced Richard Watt V in his re-furnishing of the house.

Near the door are two paintings on panel, attributed to Frans Francken the Younger and presumably purchased by Richard Watt V, representing scenes from the life of Moses: *The Crossing of the Red Sea* and *The Ark of the Covenant*.

THE STAIRCASE

There are two Victorian staircases in the domestic area of Speke, not seen by visitors, but this is the main staircase. It is undeniably a disappointment. When the Great Parlour was first built, it appears likely that a much narrower four-square stairway led to the rooms above (a remnant survives in the roof space). However, it seems extraordinary that in the mid-sixteenth century, when the west range was added, the opportunity was not taken to build something more elaborate. Clearly, visitors were not expected to use this staircase and the west range was an entirely domestic addition, not intended to make any impact after the extravagance of the Great Parlour.

On the two landings are Victorian lavatories occupying the site of the Elizabethan garderobes, which took advantage of the direct drop into the moat.

THE GALLERIES

Like the passages below, this upper tier of galleries on two sides of the courtyard, is one of Speke's unusual architectural features. The roof construction suggests that there may have been a change of plan during building, since the main trusses extend only across the width of the rooms, not across the gallery. The difference is made up by subsidiary rafters supported on blocks from the trusses. By the time the north range was added in 1598, the width of the passages was included in the plan and the trusses extend right across the width of the present building. In 1712 the agent settled an account for 'limestone att Leverpool for whitewashing and Plastering in the Galleries . . .' The decoration – partly sixteenth-century panelling heavily stained and partly painted with false timbering – dates from the Victorian period.

Although not as wide as the usual long gallery, these upper corridors would surely have been similarly used for exercising and other amusements in wet weather, as well as providing an excellent view of activities in the courtyard.

THE BLUE BEDROOM

In the 1624 inventory no fewer than 26 rooms are listed as containing a bed of some description. It is not possible always to identify existing rooms with those described, but it seems likely that this was 'Sir Thomas Gerarde's chamber' (Gerarde was a member of a neighbouring Cheshire family). It was handsomely furnished with a standing' bed hung with blue and yellow taffeta. In 1700 it was occupied by Richard Norris, the youngest of Thomas Norris's sons, and the last male member

Diogenes and Alexander; from the Mortlake tapestry, c.1700, in the Blue Bedroom

The Oak Bedroom, c.1907

of the family to inherit Speke Hall; Richard died in 1731.

Beside the Victorian fireplace is a glass panel revealing a cavity in the chimney and a spy-hole. Before the Victorian alterations to the chimney flue this may have provided one of several hideaways for priests.

FURNITURE

The half-tester bed has been rehung with blue woollen damask hangings, as described in the 1867 inventory. Like so many pieces at Speke, this Victorian bed comprises numerous continental carvings, notably a very fine seventeenth-century Flemish carving of the Last Supper on the footboard. All the furniture belongs to Richard Watt V's refurbishment, including the French eighteenth-century oak cupboard.

TAPESTRIES

The English tapestries were woven at Mortlake *c.*1700, both representing scenes from the story of Diogenes. The larger piece illustrates the philosopher's response, when the Emperor Alexander offered him assistance: 'Get Out of my light.' The second represents Diogenes claiming that Plato would not have been dependent on the hospitality of the tyrant Dionysius of Syracuse, if he had learnt to make do with field herbs, as Diogenes himself did. The central figures of these two tapestries are taken from engravings by Salvator Rosa of 1662.

THE OAK BEDROOM

The handsome proportions of this room make it the grandest of Speke's many bedrooms. In the 1624 inventory it is described as 'my Lordes Chamber' and was presumably occupied by Sir William

Norris IV. It was lavishly furnished with green and yellow damask bed-hangings and upholstered seat furniture, whilst the two window seats were fitted with cushions of cloth-of-gold and cloth-of-silver. With red and white window curtains, the room must have presented a colourful appearance.

FURNITURE

This room is furnished now as it was in Miss Watt's time. The bed is mounted with numerous pieces of continental carving, most notably a seventeenth-

Detail of the monkey border to one of the Mortlake tapestries in the Tapestry Room

century figure on the headboard, perhaps representing the Archangel Michael. In the centre is a Dutch walnut and marquetry table of the late seventeenth century. A massive German wall cupboard of the early eighteenth century with applied carvings stands between the two windows.

PICTURES

As a result of an unsubstantiated tradition that Charles I stayed here in 1630, the room has sometimes been called the Royal Bedroom. The three autotype reproductions of Van Dyck's portraits of Charles I, his Queen and his three eldest children reinforce that tradition.

Immediately outside this room, visitors should note a glazed panel, through which can be seen the ladder to the priest's hole beside the chimney of the Green Bedroom.

THE GREEN BEDROOM

This fully panelled room conceals a cavity which would have provided a hiding place for illegal priests. It is reached by a ladder (for display purposes set up permanently) in the cupboard on the left, and a tight passage between the panelling and the chimney-breast leads to a space situated above the right-hand closet, which also has access to the roof space above. Although this room forms part of William Norris's west range, the cavity may be an adaptation by Edward Norris, whose wife Margaret was an acknowledged recusant who was reported and fined for her adherence to the old religion.

The green hangings in this room have been made by volunteers, and reflect the green damask described in the 1867 inventory. At that date, it was merely called bedroom number 5, but the present name was used in Miss Watt's time.

THE TAPESTRY BEDROOM

This handsome room is situated over the gatehouse and as such is easily identifiable in the early inventories. In 1700 it was already furnished with 'hangings upon the wall', but these may have been plain woollen hangings rather than tapestries. However, tapestries were certainly hung here as part of Richard Watt V's refurbishments, and three fragments from an otherwise unknown Mortlake set of *c.*1700, have been installed following conservation. These illustrate the story of Psyche in which, having provoked the jealousy of Venus for winning the love of Cupid, she seeks the support of Juno and goes into Hades to fetch a phial of beauty from Proserpine to give to Venus.

This room is also associated with Speke's ghost story: a young mother, discovering that her husband was ruined, threw her baby out of the window into the moat and subsequently killed herself in the Great Hall. The story is said to relate to Mary Norris, but she and her son survived into maturity.

FIREPLACE

The stone fire surround is one of the few original fireplaces to survive at Speke. The plaster above shows a simple pattern of pargetting, which also occurs in the south-east corner of the courtyard, suggesting a similar, early seventeenth-century date.

FURNITURE

The tester bed is largely seventeenth-century, but the bases of the free-standing posts are Victorian replacements. The medallion on the headboard depicts St Raymund, an obscure Catalan saint who became Grand Master of the Dominican Order in 1236. The two saints depicted on either side, St Nicholas of Bari and St Margaret of Antioch, were both removed from the church calendar in 1969. The oak cradle is an entirely Victorian creation, in spite of the carved date, as are the other oak pieces here. The ivory-mounted hairbrush set bears Adelaide Watt's initials and has recently been given to Speke Hall by Tom Whatmore, the son of Miss Watt's last butler.

THE BATHROOM

This former dressing-room was converted into a bathroom only at the beginning of this century, when the heavily varnished wallpaper in the style of Willim Morris would have been hung. Tin baths of the sort displayed in the Green Bedroom would have continued in use in bedrooms, with house-maids bringing hot water in brass cans. Even in 1986 the house contained only three bathrooms.

The woven cotton 'huckaback' towels bear the initials of Richard and Adelaide Watt, the modern 'Christy' towelling being introduced only in the late nineteenth century.

Visitors are now directed down the new staircase to the Servants' Passage. Behind the glazed panel on the stairs a section of the original wattle and daub infill can be seen.

THE SERVANTS' HALL

Much conjecture relates to this room, the window of which externally takes the form of a large Gothic arch. Until the mid-nineteenth century, the room extended the full width of the range and could be entered only from the courtyard. It has been suggested, therefore, that this might be the site of the family chapel. By the sixteenth century it was not unusual for families of either faith to maintain their own chapel, but it is surprising to find so prominent a location for a Catholic chapel. The 1624 inventory mentions both an 'ould chappell' (perhaps the Gun Room), which was evidently being used as a storeroom, and a 'new Chapell'. By 1700, when the family had renounced Catholicism, there is no mention of a chapel at Speke.

In 1848 this room was being used as a laundry, and only when the new laundry was built by Richard Watt V in the Kitchen courtyard did this become the Servants's Hall. The bell-board outside summoned servants to all parts of the house.

Here are displayed an assortment of lamps and candlesticks, which in Victorian times would have been kept in the Lamp Room next door (now the ticket office), where the 'Odd Man' would have attended to them and ensured that they were ready for use each evening.

THE KITCHEN AND SCULLERY

These are in the east range, which was built in four phases, extending northwards from the original cruck-beamed wall on the south-east corner. The Scullery appears to have been added before the Kitchen, but dating of the timber suggests that they were built within a short period *c.*1600. The curious fact that the intervening wall does not follow the line of the beams is due to the wall being contemporary with the Scullery's vast sandstone chimneystack, which, like that in the Kitchen, was built later. The round-headed windows in the alcove are a later addition, perhaps inserted in the nineteenth century and taken from elsewhere.

The present arrangement of the Kitchen follows from Richard Watt V's re-equipping of the house c.1855. However, kitchen technology had developed during the intervening period and no less than four phases of cooking can be observed. The present range, astutely named 'Kooksjoie', is the most modern, dating from c.1910. It is a close range,

allowing numerous saucepans to be used at once and also enabling the smell and dirt of the coal fire to be contained. The previous range can be seen in the 1904 photograph, and its spit contraption, by William Bennett of Liverpool, survives above the warming cupboard. The earlier systems are evident in the adjoining alcove: the steel spit hanging on the wall, which would have been associated with an open grate, and the small charcoal burner under the window. This and the small hot hearth alongside provided a more intense heat, suitable for sauces rather than stews, and are an indication of the sophisticated French-style cooking in this household in the nineteenth century.

The Servants' Hall

The Kitchen

IMPLEMENTS

All the equipment on show here belonged to Miss Watt and most of it is Victorian, with the exception of the table against the courtyard wall which has a fine seventeenth-century base. Among the more unusual items are the oak jelly-stand in the far corner; the large zinc-lined container for flour and dry goods nearby; the copper *bain-marie* for sauces on the side-stove; the numerous moulds in the store cupboard; the glass butterchurn; and the cast-iron coffee grinder and percolator. It is not possible to list every item, and visitors are invited to ask the room steward about any object of interest.

This is the end of the tour of the house and visitors are asked to return across the passage to the Dairy which leads to the Dairy courtyard. Visitors should please remember to collect their belongings from the cloakroom by the door at the foot of the stairs before leaving the building.

CHAPTER TWO

HISTORY OF THE BUILDING

As one of the outstanding timber-framed buildings of the north-west, Speke was much written about in architectural literature of the nineteenth century. However, following the recent major repair programme, it has been possible to reassess the sequence of its construction in more detail, also taking advantage of scientific analysis by dendrochronology. In addition, archaeological work in recent years in the north-west corner of the site and in the East Courtyard prior to re-cobbling, has contributed to our awareness of earlier structures on the site.

These earlier buildings are mentioned in tantalisingly brief references, for instance in 1314, concerning land which 'lies in le Clogh, below the house of the said John and Nicola [Le Noreis]'. Then in 1367 Sir Henry Norris was granted a licence for an oratory at his manor house at Speke. Two more descriptive references occur *c.*1385: 'Two rooms at the end of the Hall on the west and the third of a barn at the west end . . . [and] a kiln with the fuel'; followed a few years later by a cook house with a room and the third of a barn namely the end in the east; a kiln with the fuel'. These references suggest that the site was in multiple occupation at the time.

As with all ancient timber-framed buildings, Speke's building history is a complicated mixture of additions, adaptations and accompanying losses. Furthermore, here the complexity is in part concealed by the apparent uniformity lent by the features that appear throughout: the sandstone plinth, on which the timber-framed structure is based, and by the continuous course of billeting beneath the curved cove that occurs on every elevation, as well as by the diagonal bracing and decorative use of quatrefoils.

The sequence of building broadly takes a clockwise course from the south-east corner. This account follows that route.

THE SOUTH-EAST CORNER

This section of the house, extending west to the pair of projecting bays in the centre of the south elevation, contains both the earliest and latest phases of the building of Speke as it now stands. At the eastern end is the Victorian laundry, now the Education Room, added *c.*1860 and decorated with false painted timbering. Immediately alongside this a passage runs through the wing, the western wall of which contains one of the two pairs of cruck-beams which are the remnants of an earlier hall on this site. The curved blades of the cruck-beams are visible in the roof, the western pair joining at the apex, and the next pair linked by a saddle beam which supports a king- post carrying the ridge. The timbers in the area of this second pair are scorched, suggesting that they were situated above the central open fireplace. Surviving wind-braces indicate that this hall extended by another bay in both directions. Unfortunately, the timbers did not provide adequate samples for dendrochronology, so no firm date can be given for this earliest surviving part of Speke.

The third gable from the east, set back on the line of the main frame, in fact forms the end of the east range, and was the first section of that range to be built, constituting an adaptation of the west end of the cruck hall.

THE SOUTH RANGE

Although the south range has a continuous ridge line, it nevertheless comprises two distinct phases, with the six bays of the Great Hall to the west (left) preceding the four bays to the east (right) behind the two projecting wings. The left-hand of these two wings is the earliest structure of this group, now containing the Blue Drawing Room, and then perhaps providing temporary family accommodation

The north-west corner of the Courtyard

The south range

during the building of the new Great Hall and Parlour in the 1530s. This is suggested because it comprises several reused timbers, including three of the main posts which are chamfered, indicating that originally they may have been tie-beams.

The adjoining wing on the eastern side was a quite separate build, and in the nineteenth century the ground-floor room was brick-lined to form a cellar. The quatrefoil panels are constructed of pairs of vertical timbers on the right, whilst those on the earlier wing are made up of the more conventional diagonal quarters.

The south elevation of the Great Hall itself is much altered and probably originally had only an upper row of windows, as suggested by the surviving in-filled mullions. Dendrochronology has given a date of 1530 for the felling of several timbers in this section. The porch and the large ground-floor window are later additions.

The sandstone gateway, dated on the inner side 1605, with the initials 'EN' and 'MN' for Edward Norris (1540–1606) and his wife Margaret, is not in its original position and indeed may have been reversed, since the inscription would usually be displayed outwardly. It is not known when this

part of the moat was drained, except that this took place before 1781, and it is likely that the gate was moved at the time when a new garden was being created.

The puzzling feature of the misalignment of the great sandstone chimney projecting into the Rose Garden has already been discussed in the Great Hall (see p.12). The likelihood of its being built in two phases is suggested by the projecting plinth, a detail which is not found on the adjoining hall or bay, whereas the billeted coving carved into the sandstone links precisely with the adjoining timber-framing. The gable to the south bay of the Great Hall boasts the only surviving carved bargeboard, all the others having been replaced in previous restorations.

THE GREAT PARLOUR RANGE

This section, with its quite separate roof, was built immediately after the Great Hall, dendrochronology having indicated a felling date only a year later in 1531. The large room above the Great Parlour is called 'The Great Nurserie' in the 1624 inventory, and may in fact have formed Lady Norris's apartment, its furnishings being second in value only to those of 'My Lordes Chamber'. The

Speke from the south-west; watercolour by William Herdman, 1860 (Small Dining Room)

sill to the upper window is carved with a cord motif, which is repeated on the later north end of the west range. The small sandstone porch, a later addition, carries the date 1612 and the initials of Sir William Norris IV and his wife, Eleanor Molyneux.

Although containing some of the grandest rooms in the house, the framework of this section was revealed during the recent repairs to be of surprisingly inferior quality. Contrary to the elementary rules of timber construction, the main roof trusses did not correspond with the wall-posts and in some cases were carried on the wall-plate. Jerry-building obviously flourished in Tudor times, and here may indicate that Sir William had by this stage overstretched himself and was economising.

Situated on the south-west corner, this part of the building is the most exposed to the prevailing weather and it is unsurprising that the gabled timbers have been entirely replaced. On the west elevation, the single bay of timber bracing and plaster infill panels is entirely nineteenth-century.

THE WEST RANGE

The unexpected weather-boarding on this mid-sixteenth-century elevation may have been adopted on account of its position, exposed to the prevailing and often salt-laden wind. Beneath the weather-boarding, the panels are of wattle and daub, with no external plaster, and it is likely that those sections now filled with nineteenth-century brick were also boarded originally. It was this side of the house that suffered most decay during the eighteenth century, and indeed was described as 'a complete wreck' in the mid-nineteenth century. Close inspection of the sandstone plinth on this side reveals several features that may relate to previous buildings on this site.

The west range is the largest single unit at Speke, extending through ten bays. Furthermore, its roof boasts the best continuous series of carpenter's marks, the trusses being numbered from one to ten and the purlins from one to twenty, all in Roman numerals and both sets starting from the south.

It has already been noted that the north elevation was designed to correspond with that of the Great Parlour to the south, with the exception of the north gable, which has been replaced with painted plaster. In addition, the first-floor room at the north end, 'my Lordes Chamber' (now the Oak Bedroom), may have had an oriel window on the west side, where mortises with peg holes survive. This would correspond with the 1624 inventory, which mentions window seats.

THE NORTH RANGE

The inscription over the gatehouse firmly claims this elevation as the work of Edward Norris (1540–1606). In fact it seems likely that the west range already extended three bays eastwards on this line. Not only are there breaks on both wall-plates and the courtyard base-plate at this point, but the sandstone plinth also displays a straight joint. Furthermore, the four eastern bays are considerably wider but regular at fourteen feet, and the first-floor rooms on the east end all have lower ceilings.

As on the west range, the roof slope to the courtyard side is longer to accommodate the passages, but on the north range this is achieved by the insertion of three purlins. At the west end there are clues to suggest that the roof was adapted to achieve this uniformity and hence, perhaps, Edward's claim to have built the entire length.

The timber-framing of the north elevation is comparatively plain and only modest emphasis is given to the central gatehouse with its cusped concave-sided lozenges (which also appear on the north side of the courtyard). The sandstone arch bearing the initials of Edward and his wife, Margaret Smallwood, gives weight to the centre but undoubtedly its present prominence derives from the handsome sandstone screen flanking both sides of the entrance. This appears to be a later addition and is slightly dissimilar in detail from the south gate. Perhaps it was a final flourish commissioned by the extravagant Sir William, Edward's son, who was forced to mortgage the house in 1624. The sandstone bridge was presumably built by Edward, when he created this new formal approach.

To the east of the gatehouse lies the Gothic

The inscription over the gatehouse records that Edward Norris built the north range in 1598

window already discussed in the Servants' Hall (see p.20). It forms an uncomfortable composition, with its point meeting the sill of the first-floor window. The adjoining single-storey building housed the dairy and was added c.1860. The timbers behind this roof were discovered during repairs to be free of the tar compound with which the external woodwork of Speke is now treated, suggesting that this was applied only later in the nineteenth century.

THE EAST RANGE

This range was built in three phases over a comparatively short period by Edward Norris at the end of the sixteenth century. It is now dominated by its two massive sandstone chimneys, which are later additions. The billeted coving continues here on the timber-framed portions, but otherwise this elevation has little in common with the remainder of Speke. The round-arched windows are often found in Lancashire farmhouses c.1560, usually associated with important rooms, and perhaps reused here at a later date.

Excavations in the courtyard during the course of recent building work revealed the sandstone footings of earlier structures on this site, but not in sufficient detail to suggest a plan.

THE DOVECOTE

In the north-east corner of the courtyard is the ruin of a substantial sandstone dovecote. A 'dovehouse chamber' is mentioned in the 1624 inventory, but cannot be linked specifically with this location. The sandstone revetment on which this building stands shows buttressing similar to that found on the mid-sixteenth-century west range, which may suggest that this area was being reinforced at the same time.

THE EAST MOAT BRIDGE

In 1712 there is a reference in the steward's accounts to 'Pailing the Wood Bridge'. This is followed in 1713 by an amount for 'paveinge on the stone bringe [sic]' and 'Filling rubbish at Bridge end'. These references may indicate the replacement of

The stables

a timber structure with the present bridge. The eastern section of the moat remained water-filled well into the nineteenth century.

THE STABLES

Across the east moat bridge is a small timber-framed building, which was converted by Frederick Leyland in 1868 to provide stabling for six horses. It is the truncated remnant of a much larger barn. Furthermore, it contains a pair of cruck beams, the blades of which are visible in the roof space and are of a somewhat debased quality, suggesting a comparatively late date, possibly even the seventeenth century.

THE NORTH LODGE

This lodge and its identical pair at the end of the west drive were built at the request of Frederick Leyland in 1868 to designs by the Liverpool architect Thomas Shelmerdine. The agent's correspondence at the time suggests the need to keep out unwanted visitors, particularly in the Christmas period when the hollies were vulnerable to theft and special guards were employed.

CHAPTER THREE
THE GARDEN

The garden that we now see at Speke was laid out during the brief ten-year ownership of Speke by the last Richard Watt, who died in 1865. Remarkably little is known about the sixteenth-century garden. The sandstone porch added to the Great Parlour is dated 1612, suggesting that at that date there may have been a feature such as the parterre to the south of the house. However, the date of the filling-in of the south-east section of the moat is very uncertain, except that it evidently took place before Addison's survey of 1781. The formal layout of the South Lawn shown by Addison could be the relic of a seventeenth-century scheme, of which the sandstone gateway dated 1605 may have formed a part.

Gardeners are referred to in the 1624 inventory and their equipment is listed, stored in the 'Candle Howse'. Including mole traps and a grafting saw, as well as three wheelbarrows, four spades, two rakes, three pairs of shears and four little weeding knives, the list does not seem too unlike the contents of a modern potting shed. 'One long hooke for the hopyord' relates to the hops being grown alongside the Clough, south of the orchard.

The first, albeit brief, references to gardening activity are contained in the early eighteenth-century accounts of John Wiswall, steward to Edward Norris between 1710 and 1719. In 1710 Katherine Tyrer is paid for 'weeding in Garden Courts and dressing Squares when mown', and in the same year 'seeds and little trees' are purchased from London. Potatoes, cabbages and 'colly flower' and 'sparrow grass' plants are also bought. In 1712 joiners are paid 'for making frames for Gardiners

A romantic view of the garden and south front of Speke before the 1850s restoration; watercolour by Joseph Nash, 1849

Hott bedd glasses etc.' and in 1716 peach trees were ordered.

The 1781 survey shows the moat still holding water on the eastern side, whilst early nineteenth-century watercolours seem to suggest that the western side, though drained, remained boggy and grew willow trees. Richard Watt V not only completed the draining of the moat, but also formalised the outline, creating the tiered embankments on the western side. The large pool lying to the north of the moat was also drained, allowing the west drive to be straightened with a sandstone tunnel underneath giving access to a new stream garden beyond, which is currently being replanted.

In Miss Watt's time three gardeners were employed at Speke, the head gardener being paid £1 a week, as was the gamekeeper. The same number is presently employed by the National Trust, and they have been involved in the past ten years in the extensive restoration work, putting back old paths and creating new, improving drainage throughout, and now undertaking substantial replanting schemes in the spirit of the Victorian layout of Richard Watt V. Much of this work has been assisted by donations from the National Gardens Scheme and from Trust members' Associations.

TOUR OF THE GARDEN

The notes given here initially follow a clockwise route round the house starting from the South Lawn, which is reached via the path beside the timber-framed stables.

THE SOUTH LAWN

Aerial photographs have confirmed that the moat originally extended across this lawn, completely encircling the house. However, this section appears to have been filled in at an early stage. Certainly by 1781 Addison shows the remnants of a formal parterre in this area, which may be the 'Garden Courts' and 'Squares' referred to in Wiswall's accounts at the beginning of the eighteenth century.

J. Suker's view of 1865 (Blue Drawing Room) shows this lawn outlined by a path, which has recently been reinstated, and with flower-beds on the far side. Whilst the lawn will remain open, for occasional events, the south border is being re-planted with flowering shrubs in the Victorian taste such as lilacs, spiraeas, viburnums and mop-headed hydrangeas. A young Atlantic cedar has been planted in a focal position immediately opposite the sandstone gateway from the house. Behind a grassy path meanders down to the Bund.

THE ROSE GARDEN

Situated immediately outside the Great Parlour, it is likely that this area has always formed a small private garden since the sandstone porch was added in 1612. The present layout was reinstated in 1984 after the major building repairs and was based on old photographs of *c.*1900. A series of rectangular and L-shaped beds displays alternate plantings of 'Little White Pet' and 'The Fairy', with height provided by standard roses of the same cultivars. The whole area is surrounded on two sides by modern shrub roses, such as 'Golden Wings', 'Fritz Nobis', 'Saga', 'Pearl Drift' and 'Anna Zinkeisen'. The pastel salmon pink floribunda 'Liverpool Echo' is planted in the borders directly above the moat (that newspaper having sponsored the replanting of this Rose Garden). The strongly scented white 'Margaret Merril' is well situated by the path from the house.

THE MOAT BORDERS

These borders were designed by Graham Stuart Thomas in the 1970s to complement the pink sandstone base of the old house. A background of dark foliage is provided by *Cotinus coggygria* 'Royal Purple', *Berberis thunbergii atropurpurea* and *Corylus maxima* 'Purpurea'. In the foreground are bold groups of hemerocallis, astilbes, paeonies, crinums and sidalcea.

The formal rectangle of the west moat, part of Richard Watt V's refurbishment of the 1850s, is overhung by a rather older evergreen holm oak. Open-air concerts or plays are occasionally held here in summer. In spring the bank of the north moat is studded with fritillaries.

*Speke from the south-east; painting by J. Suker, c.1865
(Blue Drawing Room)*

THE NORTH LAWN

The typical Victorian evergreen borders are sheltered by clumps of Corsican pine with occasional
double red hawthorns and yellow-flowered labur-
nums in-between for late spring colour. The tall
hybrid hollies, *Ilex* × *altaclerensis*, clipped in the
traditional manner, are also a feature. Dramatic
change in foliage is provided by groups of yuccas
and pampas grass. Gradual replanting will be
undertaken in these borders to replace the *Rhododen-
dron ponticum*.

In the lawn itself are naturalised areas of heather,
indicating an extremely acid soil, and perhaps
representing a relic of the original heathland on the
site of Stockton's Wood nearby.

THE STREAM GARDEN

This recently replanted area is approached via the
sandstone tunnel in the dell on the west side of the
North Lawn. The whole site formed a long pond
until it was drained in the mid-nineteenth century,
and it is now being restored with a planting scheme
in the colourful taste of that period. Deciduous and
evergreen azaleas and hybrid rhododendrons are
interplanted with deciduous flowering shrubs such
as amelanchier, philadelphus, spiraea, corylopsis
and viburnums. Ferns, rodgersias and other damp-
loving plants are being established by the water's
edge.

The upper walk of the Stream Garden, which has
been planted to create a dark yew tunnel, leads on to
the west drive, at the end of which there used to
stand a black and white lodge, a pair to that at the
north entrance. Both these lodges were built in 1868
during Leyland's tenancy.

THE CLOUGH

A path opposite the yew tunnel leads southwards into the Clough, a woodland area which has provided a sheltered setting for the buildings on this site since at least 1314, when the name is first mentioned. The southern section was felled by the Air Ministry in 1942 and sycamore suckers had spread in the interval, but much replanting has recently taken place, mostly of beech and oak. In spring this area is a mass of bluebells, which were already a feature in Victorian times and are depicted in watercolours in the house.

THE BUND

The paths through the Clough all lead to the Bund, the massive earth embankment built in 1967 to protect Speke Hall from the noise and sight of aircraft taxiing to and fro while Liverpool airport was transferred from the west to the east side of Speke Hall. Part of the taxiway is on land owned by the National Trust, which was leased temporarily for the purpose of the transfer, and in due course the Trust hopes to reinstate the historic link between

Speke Hall and the Mersey shore. A path runs along the top of the Bund, reached by steps, and from there on a clear day magnificent views can be obtained of the Liverpool city skyline, including its two cathedrals, and across the Mersey to the Ellesmere Port oil terminal and the Welsh hills in the distance beyond.

THE ORCHARD

The area currently planted with fruit trees, immediately opposite the stable building, was formally the site of a large U-shaped range of farm buildings. These were demolished only in the 1880s when Miss Watt built a massive new home farm further east. Another of Miss Watt's ambitious schemes was to build an extensive range of hot-houses on this site, including peach and vine houses, but this was never executed.

Previously Speke's orchard lay between the South Lawn and the River Mersey, alongside the hop-yard. To the north of the old farm buildings lay the Swine Pasture, now the visitors' car-park.

STOCKTON'S WOOD

A deed of 1385 refers to 'the heath called spekgreves' and it seems that the area of Stockton's Wood survived as heath until the early nineteenth century. The name Stockton appears first in 1825, and the area was probably planted with trees then, specifically as coverts for shooting over. During the Second World War clearings were created within the wood, where Lockheed-Hudsons and other aircraft shipped from America were stored prior to assembly by the RAF. Packing cases of aircraft parts stood along the Walk. More recently both sides of the Walk have been planted with bold clumps of daffodils in the Victorian style, a project which has been undertaken by volunteers from the Merseyside Volunteers Group.

The rose garden outside the Great Parlour

CHAPTER FOUR
THE ESTATE

The dramatic changes of the twentieth century have almost completely obliterated all traces of the Norris estate which survived largely intact until the 1920s. No early maps of Speke and its surrounds have so far been discovered but the 1781 survey by Addison probably records a layout that was already established in the seventeenth century. This and the sale particulars drawn up shortly thereafter describe the substantial estate which had been acquired during three centuries by the Norris family, and which by 1795 amounted to some 2,400 acres. At this date it comprised a home farm, known as the demesne and amounting to some 850 acres, and 27 tenanted smallholdings varying in size from five acres to 150 and all with their associated buildings.

The Norris family is first mentioned at Speke in 1314, but ownership of the manor was then divided between different families. The marriage of Sir Henry Norris to Alice Erneys c.1390 secured further property for the Norrises, but it was not until the sixteenth century that their ownership of the township of Speke was complete. Sir Thomas Norris's rental of 1468 does not specify all acreages but does show that their land was made up in part of strips in open fields, as well as the enclosed fields near the hall and some land outside the Speke township. A later

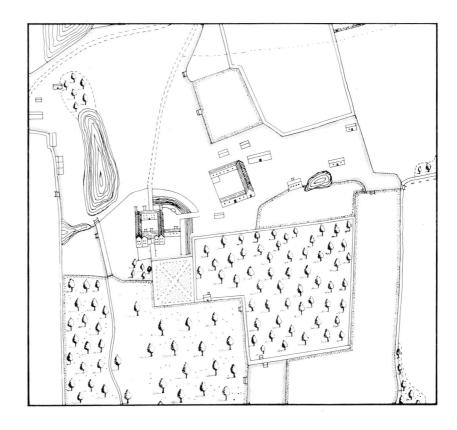

The 1781 survey of the Speke estate by Thomas Addison

note on the document mentions 'ye Wynde mylne' and by 1650, when the sequestration documents were drawn up, the estate boasted two windmills and two watermills, the latter probably at Garston.

Much information about the workings of the estate can be gleaned from the historical records, in addition to the 1468 rental already mentioned. These include the three inventories of 1524, 1624 and 1700 and the accounts of John Wiswall. The accumulation of the estate is less clear but the earliest description, in the Domesday Book of 1086, recorded that in 1066: 'Uctred held Spec. There 2 caracuates of land. It was worth 64 pence.' Given the easy terrain of Speke (a caracuate being a variable amount based on the area that could be ploughed in a year using one plough), Uctred's estate may already have amounted to over 200 acres. The fact that Speke was situated in the Royal Forest of Lancashire does not indicate that the area was wooded, but rather refers to rights and obligations pertaining there, especially as regards hunting and the use of timber within the area. In fact in 1275 Speke is described broadly as being 'wood, plain and meadow'.

Some of the land was heath or moorland, and peat extraction for the landlord was one of the duties or boons undertaken by tenants, as listed in Thomas Norris's 1468 rental: 'every man a day to delfe Turves'. These duties illustrate the agricultural activity of the time and included a day with a plough, a day with a muckcart, the supply of a horse for a day, the fetching of hay, reaping at harvest. Non-performance of such boons led to payment of a fine and they were still being practised in 1693 in the form of coal-carrying, haymaking and reaping.

The scale of farming in the period that Speke was built is illustrated in Henry Norris's inventory of 1524, which identified 16 acres of wheat, 33 of barley and 20 of oats. Twenty draught oxen and 5 work horses are listed, along with 61 cattle, 60 sheep and 28 pigs. The nature of the land, described in the 1795 sale particulars as 'a deep and red loam, mixed with sand', was ideal for cultivation, and early fertilising with marle is suggested by the reference to Richard le Marler in 1329. By 1624 14 marle carts

are listed in the inventory, and the numerous residual ponds created by the extraction of this limey subsoil are shown on the 1781 survey.

In 1624 a considerable quantity of poultry is being looked after by Elizabeth Hauchmoughe: 28 capons, 56 hens, a cock, 3 turkeys, 18 ducks and 12 geese. At the same time, mention is made of the 'Dove Howse' and repairs to the pigeon house occur frequently in Wiswall's accounts, which also record the use of pigeon dung as a fertiliser.

Further variety to the diet would have been provided by fish from the numerous ponds and the moat, all of which were regularly stocked with carp, tench and perch. In addition, the Mersey was regularly fished, and there is a reference in 1698 to the 'vast numbers of Salmon Trout' and to one of the Norrises catching '3 or 4 a week at a fishing'. Both the 1624 and 1700 inventories mention fishing nets, which would have been used in the Mersey.

The 1795 sale particulars emphasised that the estate was well suited to game, although the claim that it was 'perhaps the most eligible situation in the Kingdom for Hunting and Shooting' must be deemed an early example of estate agents' hyperbole. With an eye to the commercial interest, the same particulars also suggested that the estate might be converted to a colliery, since active coalpits existed nearby. Although the Watt family did not develop this enterprise, a sandstone quarry was certainly opened to the north of the demesne land.

The estate purchased by Richard Watt I in 1795 remained intact up to the death of Miss Watt. Her will expressed the wish that the estate 'should be maintained and upheld in the best order'. However, in 1929 a portion was sold by the trustees to Liverpool City Council for the development of an aerodrome to the west of Speke Hall and shortly after the remainder was also sold. Only the drive and 27 acres of garden passed with the hall to the National Trust in 1943. Recently, however, the Trust has purchased Stockton's Wood and some of the immediately adjoining farmland in order to secure the traditional setting of the hall. In this respect, the views from the hall are also important and the Trust is concerned to ensure that future developments in the immediate neighbourhood are in sympathy with the historic setting of Speke Hall.

CHAPTER FIVE

THE OWNERS OF SPEKE

THE NORRIS FAMILY

The Norris family first acquired overall control of Speke through the marriage of Sir Henry Norris with Alice Erneys, which took place c.1390. This was one of many shrewd marriages by successive generations which enabled the Norris family to establish and maintain themselves as substantial property owners, and to play a significant part in the life of the region.

According to the Domesday Book, the manor of Speke was held in 1066 by Uctred, a Saxon, but was subsequently presented to Count Roger of Poitou, a Norman follower of William the Conqueror. For the next hundred years the issue of ownership is complicated. Under the feudal system all land belonged in theory to the King; in practice land was granted by him to tenants-in-chief, who in turn granted tenures and sub-tenures. By 1170 Speke was part of the Royal Forest of Lancashire, though actual tenure was in the hands of the Molyneuxs, one of the most powerful local families, who were to retain nominal overlordship until the late sixteenth century.

In the early thirteenth century the manor was divided into two parts, with one half being granted to Sir Patrick de Hazelwall and the other half to Robert Erneys of Chester. Sir Patrick had two daughters who married brothers, Alan and John le Noreis. By 1317 John le Noreis was in sole possession of the Hazelwall half of the manor and from 1332 he leased the Erneys' land. John and his wife, Nicola, had a house above the Clough at Speke by 1314, and from them descended the line of Norrises who were to live at Speke until the eighteenth century. The two halves of the manor were finally united in Norris ownership by the

(Right)   Henry and Clemence Norris, from their brasses in Childwall church

marriage of Sir Henry and Alice. Furthermore, it was a younger son of this couple who founded the Rycote branch of the Norreys family (retaining the old spelling), who provided courtiers, statesmen, admirals and soldiers for the Tudor monarchs and went on to build magnificent houses at Rycote in Oxfordshire and Ockwells in Berkshire.

Following the death of Alice's brother c.1396 she and Henry inherited the last portion of the manor of Speke. Ten years earlier a 1385 rental had referred to

the buildings at Speke: 'two rooms at the end of the Hall on the west and . . . a barn at the west end . . . a kiln . . .'. Whether the moated site had been created by this date is a matter of conjecture. The next reference to the Norris holdings at Speke is contained in the rental drawn up by Thomas in 1468. His wife, Lettice Norris, brought him further property in West Derby.

Thomas's son, the first of six William Norrises, established the family reputation on the battlefield, being knighted after the Battle of Stoke in 1487. A generation later, in 1513, three of his sons – Henry, William and Edward – were all fighting at the Battle of Flodden in which the Scottish King was killed. Henry, who succeeded to Speke in 1506, is commemorated with his wife Clemence by brasses in Childwall church. In 1544 Henry's son, William Norris II, was also fighting for his King north of the border, in Lord Hertford's expedition. The plunder

William Norris II, who inherited Speke in 1524, is commemorated in the Great Parlour overmantel, flanked by his two wives, with their nineteen children below. He built the Great Parlour and the Great Hall in the 1530s

brought back by this Norris included folios belonging to the Abbot of Cambuskeneth, which he wished 'to remain at Speke for an heirloom'.

William Norris II inherited Speke in 1524 and was knighted in 1531, about the time he began work on the magnificent rooms in the south range that we see today – the Great Hall and Great Parlour. The only portrait of this William is contained in the Great Parlour overmantel, where he is depicted in the centre, flanked by his two wives, with his nineteen children below and his father in the left-hand panel. His enthusiasm for the then fashionable subject of genealogy is also demonstrated by the 'genealogical declaration' which he compiled in 1563. He continued the expansion of the Norris estate, buying and exchanging land so that when he died in 1568 he was recorded as having property in Garston, Hale, Halewood, Allerton and Much Woolton. It is William II who firmly established his branch of the Norris family at Speke and in 1544 began the long family tradition of representing Liverpool in Parliament.

His eldest son, William III, died at the Battle of Pinkie in 1547 and so it was his second son, Edward, who inherited in 1568 and finally completed the building of Speke, adding the north and east ranges. The late sixteenth century was a difficult period for the family. The accession of Elizabeth I in 1558 saw the virtual victory of Protestantism in England, but Lancashire remained a stronghold of the old faith. After Elizabeth's excommunication in 1570 English Catholics were increasingly viewed as subversives and potential traitors. Edward appears to have kept quiet about his religious beliefs, although in 1586 he was reported for having harboured a priest, one Richard Brittain. (The priest's holes at Speke may date from this period.) Edward's wife, Margaret Smallwood, was a more outspoken recusant, on whose account he had to pay a fine of £15 in 1598.

Edward was succeeded in 1606 by his eldest son, William IV, who had been made a Knight of the Bath at the coronation of James I and who had married Eleanor, daughter and heir apparent of Sir Richard Molyneux of Sefton. Their initials appear on the little sandstone porch, dated 1612, in front of the Great Parlour, and it seems likely that the couple was responsible for the lavish furnishings of Speke

The initials of William Norris IV and his wife Eleanor appear on the little sandstone porch, dated 1612, adjoining the Great Parlour

When William Norris V died in 1651, he was succeeded by his second son, Thomas. Although Thomas was the first head of the family to adopt Protestantism, he too was described as being a supporter of the King and fined. His inheritance at that time included 'the manor and capital messuage of Speke with the demesnes thereof, three cottages, two windmills, two watermills and land of the yearly value of £224 5s 8d' as well as rents amounting to a further £70.

It remained for the next generation to re-establish the family reputation and to resume their position in Liverpool. The eldest son, another Thomas, married the daughter of Sir Willoughby Aston and served as MP for Liverpool in 1689 and 1690 and Sheriff of Lancashire in 1696. The next brother, Sir William VI, was MP for Liverpool when he was appointed Ambassador to the Court of the Mogul Emperor Aurangzeb in 1698. He was finally received by the Emperor in April 1701, when he presented him with 'quantities of cloth, clocks and watches, looking-glasses, "ribbed hubble-bubbles", tea-pots, "essence violls", double microscopes, six

described in the 1624 inventory, which was drawn up in order to secure a loan. Described both as a 'gallant and high spirited soldier' and a 'quarrelsome spendthrift', William IV found himself before the Star Chamber for striking a Protestant magistrate who had been enquiring into his attendance at church. The huge fine of £1,000 was later reduced to £250. Needing to raise money, he sold parts of the estate, and tried to dispose of his property at Blacon which was occupied by his son, William V, who refused to move until he was paid his promised annuity. William V was also a convicted recusant, paying double taxes, but in spite of his father's efforts to disinherit him, he was finally able to reclaim Speke in 1634. He appears to have played little part in the Civil War, although he contributed timber to the Royalists for the rebuilding of Liverpool in 1645. His eldest son, Edward, was an active Royalist and as Governor held Liverpool for a period on behalf of the King.

Sir William Norris VI, who led an embassy to the Court of the Mogul Emperor Aurangzeb in 1698

"extraordinary christiall reading-glasses with fish-skin cases" and an eight-foot telescope'. Despite these gifts, his mission proved a futile one, undermined by the machinations of his fellow countrymen in England and India, and he died on the return trip in 1702. He had been accompanied by his younger brother, Edward, who brought home a cargo valued at 87,000 rupees on Sir William's account, which proved a fertile source of litigation among the family.

A letter from their widowed mother Katherine in 1705 to their youngest brother Richard provides an insight into the more everyday concerns of life in early eighteenth-century Lancashire:

Last week I wrot to some of your frinds in westminster & truly on[e] letter a weeak is as much as I like to wright for haveing laid by my Specticals I question whether if my wrighting can be red, for truly when I have wright I can hardly read it my Self, we are very well at present but last weeak was in a littell fear on[e] of the wemen servants was not well and we thought it might have bin smale poxx for Elizar Spencers chilldren has them & most houses in town whar is chilldren & the old folk hath the Ague . . .

Edward was a doctor and became a Fellow of the Royal College of Physicians in 1716. Like his elder brothers, he was elected MP for Liverpool, from 1715 to 1722. Edward died in 1726, leaving Speke to Richard, the last of the four brothers to inherit the property. Richard also played his part in the local community, becoming Mayor of Liverpool in 1700, MP between 1708 and 1710, and Sheriff of Lancashire in 1718. When he died in 1731 without an heir, the estate passed to the daughter of his eldest brother, Thomas. Mary Norris thus became a substantial heiress, and the future of Speke depended on her finding a husband.

THE BEAUCLERKS

It must have seemed probable that the Norris line at Speke would shortly terminate altogether, when at the comparatively advanced age of 36 Mary Norris contracted a marriage in 1736 with Lord Sidney Beauclerk, a son of the Duke of St Albans and grandson of Nell Gwyn. Her husband made no secret of the fact that he was fortune hunting and

Topham Beauclerk; pastel by Francis Cotes, 1756

had earlier almost persuaded the aged but wealthy Lady Betty Germain into a marriage, from which she only escaped by paying him off with £1,000. He and Mary must have made an unlikely pair: she was described as having 'no notion of a joke . . . and . . . a mighty unpliable understanding', whilst Lady Mary Wortley Montagu wrote of him as 'Nell Gwynn in person with the sex altered, [who] occasioned such fracas amongst the ladies of Daventry that it passes belief'. From another contemporary he earned the epithet 'worthless Sidney'.

Evidently he could be an engaging personality to male as well as female companions, so much so that the MP for Windsor, Richard Topham, was persuaded to bequeath him his substantial estates at Windsor and Clewer. In due course, he became MP for Windsor himself but died young in 1744. He had bestowed the name of his benefactor on the only child of the marriage, Topham, born in 1739.

This young man at the age of 17 met and won the lasting friendship of Dr Johnson who, according to Boswell, 'delighted in the good qualities of Beauclerk, and hoped to correct the evil'. Topham seems to have combined a delight in cultivated society with a disregard for social niceties, to the extent of his personal habits being described as more suited to a beggar or a gypsy. He admitted himself to 'insuperable idleness', but mixed with the great minds of the period, including Burke, Goldsmith and Reynolds, and was one of the outstanding bibliophiles of the era, building up a collection of over 30,000 volumes for which he commissioned Robert Adam to design him a library for his house in Bloomsbury.

It is difficult to associate this dilettante figure with Speke Hall, which in the mid-eighteenth century would have been utterly unfashionable, and uncomfortable too. We know that he visited his Lancashire estates from time to time, on one occasion diverting en route to meet Rousseau in Ashbourne. However, it seems unlikely that he ever lived at Speke permanently and, having in 1768 married Lady Diana Bolingbroke, a daughter of the 3rd Duke of Marlborough, they settled at Thanet House in Great Russell Street in London.

His wife was another fashionable figure, an artist of some repute and greatly admired by Horace Walpole, who hung her paintings in the little hexagonal 'Beauclerc Closet' at Strawberry Hill. She is probably best known now for her rather sentimental designs of Neo-classical reliefs for Wedgwood's Jasper ware.

Topham died in 1780 at the age of 40, his early enthusiasms having already turned to misanthropy. His son Charles was then aged only six and, on coming of age in 1795, he immediately set about selling his Lancashire estates and thereby finally brought to a close the continuous ownership of Speke by one family extending back over four and a half centuries. Ironically, one of the most significant surviving documents relating to Speke's history, Addison's survey of 1781, which is the earliest known plan of Speke Hall and its surroundings, was commissioned during the period of Charles's minority. As to the state of Speke Hall itself by the end of the eighteenth century, that was recorded later by a member of the Watt family who purchased it.

THE WATT FAMILY

The Richard Watt who purchased Speke Hall in 1795 epitomises the rags-to-riches tradition. Born in Standish, near Wigan, he had started off as a lad by helping to drive the only Hackney carriage service in Liverpool. Encouraged by his employer to attend evening school, he went on to find a position on a ship to Jamaica. There he made his fortune, as well as acquiring a sugar plantation at St George's Plain. The blackamoor head that features on his coat of arms acknowledges the source of his wealth. By the 1770s he was back in Liverpool running a substantial shipping company in the fastest-growing port in Britain and the heart of the West Indies trade. Such was his wealth that, after building himself a house at Oak Hill in 1773, he was able in 1783 to purchase a 2,500-acre estate at Bishop Burton in Yorkshire and finally, just before his death, he also became the owner of Speke Hall and its estate of similar size.

The Watts appear to have been a close-knit family and Richard took as partners his nephews, another Richard Watt (II) and Richard Walker. It was the son of the former, his great-nephew and godson, Richard Watt III, who was to be the chief beneficiary of his will, inheriting both estates along

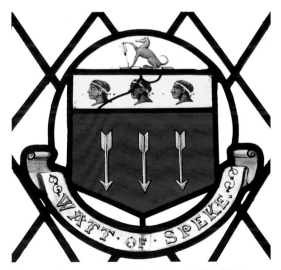

The coat of arms used by Richard Watt I. The blackamoor heads acknowledge the origin of his wealth in Jamaican sugar plantations

with the plantation in Jamaica and £100,000. The will also conveyed to him the 'Negroes and other slaves together with the offspring and increase of the females of such slaves cattle plantation utensils hereditaments and real estate' in Jamaica. As a beneficiary of the system, Richard Watt III opposed the emancipation of slaves and in 1807 refused to vote for Wilberforce in Yorkshire.

Richard Watt III was only ten when his great-uncle died in 1796. Richard's father, who had settled at Bishop Burton, managed both estates on his son's behalf, but died at the early age of 52, leaving two orphan sons, Richard and Francis. They appear to have been brought up by their maternal aunt, Mary Greenup, and a beloved nanny, Elizabeth Martin, who was later to be generously remembered in Richard's will.

The house at Speke which Richard inherited was later described by him as 'very much destroyed by the people (farmers and others) that the Beauclerk family allowed to live there'. His coming of age in 1807, followed by his marriage a year later to Hannah Burns, prompted substantial refurbishments at Speke. George Bullock and Matthew Gregson, two well-known Liverpool furniture designers, were involved, and several rooms were completely refurnished, including the Great Hall, Drawing Room and a number of bedrooms. However, in 1812 this new furniture, described as 'but just finished in great taste, and never has been used', was abruptly sold. The reason for this change of plan is unknown, but it would seem that thereafter their home was at Bishop Burton.

Set in lush, rolling meadows south of Beverley, Bishop Burton provided ideal conditions for Richard to develop his passion for breeding race-horses. In 1813 he had his first major success, when Altisidora won the St Leger, a race he went on to win a further three times. A pub in the village still bears the name, but his chief breeding sire was Blacklock, whose skeleton he later kept on display at Bishop Burton and which survived intact until the 1950s, when it was finally buried.

Known as Dickie, Richard Watt III was described as 'a little man, very choleric, but quite the gentleman in demeanour and manners'. His marriage to Hannah brought them thirteen children, but she died producing the last in 1828. Even in the hard-drinking world in which he lived, Dickie's circle at Bishop Burton was notorious for its

The tomb of Richard Watt I; by John Bacon the Younger, 1796 (Standish church, Lancashire)

The derelict west range, c.1848; watercolour by J. Dodd

drunkenness, according to an account in the *Sporting Times*. Furthermore, after the death of his wife, he had acquired another companion, nicknamed 'Chunee' on account of her size, after the elephant of that name which was one of the sights of London.

Following the family tradition, the eldest son had been named Richard (IV). Little is known of him except that he appears to have married beneath himself, choosing Jane Bland, a housemaid at Bishop Burton. They went to live at Speke Hall but not long after he died at the early age of 27, leaving a daughter, Sarah, and son, the last Richard Watt (V). Perhaps surprisingly, the upbringing of the two children was left to their mother, who subsequently remarried and settled in Liverpool. Richard Watt III's will specified that his grandson should be educated at some 'respectable collegiate school (not being either Westminster, Harrow or Eton)', but by the time the will was read, in 1855, Richard Watt V was 20.

Before this date, it appears that Richard Watt III had already transferred Speke Hall to his eldest son, Richard IV, but in his will he left the contents of both Speke and Bishop Burton to his second son, Francis, who also inherited the Bishop Burton property and undertook the rebuilding of that according to his grandfather's will. It was therefore an empty Speke Hall that Richard Watt V took possession of in 1856.

During Richard V's minority Speke had been leased to a timber merchant, Joseph Brereton, and parts of the hall were described by a visitor as 'grievously neglected, until it has become a complete ruin . . . mouldings from the oak wainscot are crumbling . . . and the ivy has in many places forced itself through from the outside'. Nicholson's drawing of the 1820s (Small Dining Room) gives a romantic impression of the house in this state of neglect, which seems to have affected chiefly the western side of the house. By this time, tastes had changed, and Speke was now much admired and often painted for its ancient and picturesque qualities. Another visitor, in 1853, was the author of *Uncle Tom's Cabin*, Harriet Beecher Stowe, who commented on 'the snowy sanded floor and resplendent polished copper' in the kitchen of Joseph Brereton, whom she described as 'a bachelor who lives there very retired and employs himself much in reading'. Some of his books survive in the Library today.

In 1856, the year that he reached his majority, Richard Watt V married Adelaide Hignett of Chester and together they embarked on the not inconsiderable task of restoring and re-furnishing Speke. No designer's names are associated with this refurbishment and it would appear that they turned to the numerous furniture warehouses already established in Liverpool and London to supply the needs of the burgeoning middle classes. The great quantity of heavily carved oak furniture, and the equally ornate tulipwood suite in the Blue Drawing Room, are typical of this taste and were designated by Richard in his will to pass with the property as heirlooms. This will became effective all too soon, as tragedy struck again when he died at the age of 30 at Cowes, when just about to embark on his new yacht for the West Indies. His wife had already died in 1861, prompting a friend to write of her: 'How many happy days we passed in your noble mansion, where all received such a warm welcome from your kind self and him who loved you so dearly.' In spite of this apparent fondness, Richard's will contains the curious instruction that no member of his wife's family should become his daughter's guardian or husband.

Once again Speke was inherited by a child, a daughter Adelaide, who went to Scotland to be brought up by her great-uncle, James Sprot. For once, however, this period of minority brought enhancement rather than neglect, as Speke was let to Frederick Leyland.

FREDERICK LEYLAND

In 1867, when Leyland leased Speke, he was 36 and had been manager of the Bibby shipping line for three years. Rising from humble beginnings, at his death he owned his own shipping line, a collection of Old Masters and had a reputation as among the most discerning patrons of contemporary artists of his era.

Leyland was born in 1831 and at the age of fourteen was brought to the attention of John Bibby by his mother, who ran a pie shop in Liverpool. The Bibbys had a number of business interests, including a small fleet of sailing ships, and Leyland entered the shipping office as a clerk. He was industrious and ambitious and soon secured a place in the Bibbys' private office. He quickly made himself indispensable and furthered his own position by persuading the Bibbys to let him take shares in some of their ships, which he paid for out of his profits. He was very successful and was instrumental in moving the firm into the development of steamship services. In 1864, they appointed him manager of the shipping business and when family difficulties arose in 1872, he stepped in and took over the firm, which he renamed the Leyland Line. His main trade was with the Mediterranean, and his meticulous attention to detail ensured that the business went from strength to strength.

During his first few months at Speke, Leyland carried out considerable work to the interior of the house, redecorating the Blue Drawing Room and restoring the corridors and ground-floor rooms of

The chimney-piece in the Billiard Room is one of several introduced by Leyland

the western and north-western ranges, where the old kitchen became the Billiard Room and the scullery the Library. The alterations were completed in the best antiquarian style, inspired by original motifs and carvings found elsewhere in the house.

Among the more striking features of the Leyland redecoration are the chimney-pieces he introduced in the Morning Room, Billiard Room and Oak Bedroom. The trailing ivy motif on them is said to have been copied from a reputedly seventeenth-century fireplace in a nearby house, but it has a decidedly modern, Arts and Crafts flavour. For all Leyland's respect for the Tudor origins of Speke, he was also prepared to introduce contemporary decoration, most notably William Morris's 'Trellis', 'Daisy' and 'Pomegranate' wallpapers.

Leyland had a long-standing interest in the arts. His first and greatest love was music, having been given a piano when a boy; indeed, he would like to have become a professional concert pianist. His fondness for pictures also developed at an early age. As a young clerk he visited Hart Hill, John Bibby's home, and was scathing about his employer's taste in paintings. When his business success provided him with the wealth to do so, he began his own collection. Not only did he acquire early Italian and North European Old Masters, but he commissioned and bought work from contemporary artists.

Leyland was to become one of the greatest, and most demanding, patrons of Rossetti in the painter's later years. In August 1868 Rossetti was invited to stay at Speke, which he thought 'a glorious old house, full of interest in every way'. However, the visit was not a success, as the chloral Rossetti was starting to take for his insomnia made him poor company, and it was not repeated.

A much more frequent visitor to Speke was J. A. M. Whistler, who stayed regularly between 1869 and 1875. Whistler encouraged Leyland to buy Spanish Old Masters (in particular by Velázquez) and in August 1870 was commissioned to paint a full-length portrait of him in the same style (now in the Freer Art Gallery, Washington), which was hanging, uncompleted, at Speke in October 1871. The following month Whistler began work at Speke on a companion portrait of Leyland's wife

Leyland's estranged wife Frances appears in the foreground of Whistler's 1870 etching of Speke (shown in reverse)

Frances (Frick Art Gallery, New York), which is one of his masterpieces. It was during a visit to Speke in 1870 that he took up etching again, scraping a view of the house which includes the strangely isolated figure of Mrs Leyland in the foreground. Whistler was here perhaps hinting at the growing rift between the Leylands, in which he took the side of Frances Leyland. By 1877 the marriage had broken down completely and, with typical mischief, Rossetti began spreading rumours that Whistler and Mrs Leyland were planning to elope. An enraged Leyland, who had already spectacularly fallen out with Whistler over the decoration of the 'Peacock Room' in his London house, threatened to 'publicly horsewhip' the artist, if he ever came near his wife again.

When the lease to Speke expired in 1877, Leyland moved to nearby Woolton Hall, but in later years spent more time away from Liverpool. He died of a heart attack in 1892 at the age of 61. His collection of paintings was sold, the interiors of his London house were soon dispersed or later destroyed, and the restoration at Speke remains as his only surviving *in situ* work.

RECENT HISTORY

During Adelaide's minority, the estate was managed on behalf of her guardian by an agent, George Whitley. The very detailed and almost daily correspondence between Whitley and Mr Sprot throws an informative light not just on the activities of the tenants and events in Liverpool, but also on the nature of the man who was moulding Adelaide's character. The numerous cottages on the estate required modernising but Mr Sprot apparently 'did not approve of Parlours for poor people' and when required by the authorities to improve the sanita-

Adelaide Watt; engraving after C. W. Walton (Small Dining Room)

tion, his agent wrote to him, 'The Philistines are upon us.' The agent was instructed to seek economies throughout, including on the Jamaica estate where 'even rat traps are sent as a matter of course as not obtainable abroad on favourable terms'. At the same time modernisation and repair work was being carried out on the estate and in 1872 a new church was built at Speke as a memorial to Richard Watt V. Every detail of the building, from initial plans down to the gravel of the entrance path, had to be approved by Mr Sprot, and Adelaide brought with her the same requirements for careful economy and absolute control, which extended to giving the tenants instructions in how to place their vote at elections.

Adelaide's careful tenure of Speke saw no major changes in the hall, but she embarked almost immediately on the building of the massive new home farm complex, no doubt inspired by agricultural developments she had witnessed in East Lothian. As previously with her guardian, the agent, now Mr Graves, had to seek her approval for the price and quality of every item pertaining to this range, built in sandstone and rather more substantial than the hall itself.

Adelaide never married and when not at Speke, she was visiting relatives on her father's side of the family. One great-aunt, Charlotte Fane, seems to have been a valued companion whom she commemorated in a series of stained-glass windows in Bishop Burton church 'in grateful recollection of good counsels and just works'. At the same time, her strong sense of history and of the value of Speke prompted her to seek out members of the original Norris family who built the house, and to name three of them in her will as trustees to enjoy the benefit of Speke for a period of 21 years. Even when this will was being drawn up, however, in 1918, she was aware of the pressures of development from the expanding city of Liverpool and she included a secondary devise to the National Trust 'in case future changes in the environs may be such that the owner or occupier of the estate might cease to care to reside there'. Adelaide died in 1921 and during the period of trusteeship the estate was sold. The site of Chapel Farm quickly became Liverpool's proudest new development of the 1930s, an aerodrome,

The Great Hall c.1907

with the old farm buildings converted to hangers and the farmhouse providing the terminal.

The hall passed to the National Trust in 1943 with a requirement under her will that it 'shall always be maintained and upheld in the best order and condition'. Only a small financial endowment accompanied the gift, and Speke was therefore leased to Liverpool City Council which duly opened it to the public. Between 1976 and 1986, the lease passed to Merseyside County Council, which embarked on a massive restoration programme, during which the entire roof was repaired and much work to the timber frame undertaken. With the demise of Merseyside County Council, the man-

agement was taken over by the National Trust, which receives an annual subvention from the National Museums, Liverpool. During the course of the repair programme, the decision was taken that the exterior of the building should continue to be painted in the black and white 'magpie' tradition of the nineteenth century, complementing both the interiors and the surrounding gardens which all derive their present appearance from the Victorian era. Nevertheless, Speke Hall is above all outstanding for having survived, despite so many periods of neglect, as a marvellously complete Tudor timber-framed building.

THE NORRISES AND BEAUCLERKS

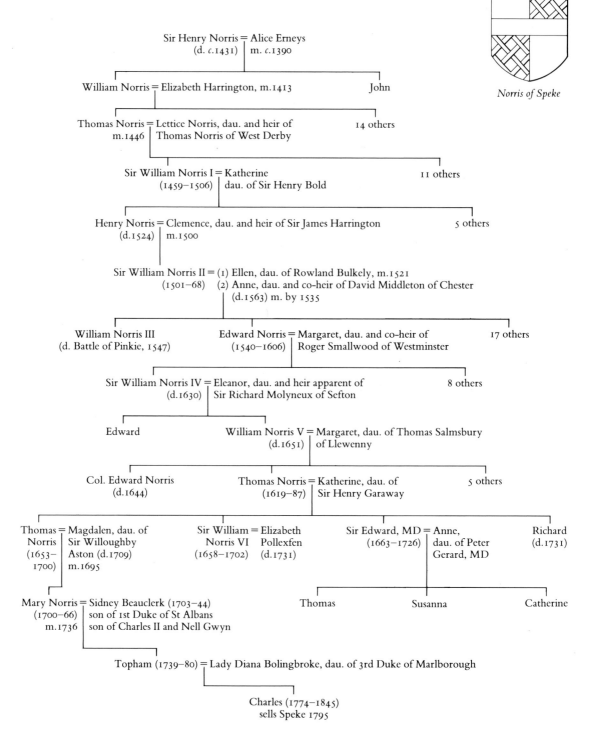

Norris of Speke

Sir Henry Norris = Alice Erneys
(d. *c*.1431) | m. *c*.1390

William Norris = Elizabeth Harrington, m.1413   John

Thomas Norris = Lettice Norris, dau. and heir of   14 others
m.1446 | Thomas Norris of West Derby

Sir William Norris I = Katherine   11 others
(1459–1506) | dau. of Sir Henry Bold

Henry Norris = Clemence, dau. and heir of Sir James Harrington   5 others
(d.1524) | m.1500

Sir William Norris II = (1) Ellen, dau. of Rowland Bulkely, m.1521
(1501–68)   (2) Anne, dau. and co-heir of David Middleton of Chester
(d.1563) m. by 1535

William Norris III   Edward Norris = Margaret, dau. and co-heir of   17 others
(d. Battle of Pinkie, 1547)   (1540–1606) | Roger Smallwood of Westminster

Sir William Norris IV = Eleanor, dau. and heir apparent of   8 others
(d.1630) | Sir Richard Molyneux of Sefton

Edward   William Norris V = Margaret, dau. of Thomas Salmsbury
(d.1651) | of Llewenny

Col. Edward Norris   Thomas Norris = Katherine, dau. of   5 others
(d.1644)   (1619–87) | Sir Henry Garaway

Thomas = Magdalen, dau. of   Sir William = Elizabeth   Sir Edward, MD = Anne,   Richard
Norris | Sir Willoughby   Norris VI | Pollexfen   (1663–1726) | dau. of Peter   (d.1731)
(1653– | Aston (d.1709)   (1658–1702) | (d.1731) | Gerard, MD
1700) | m.1695

Mary Norris = Sidney Beauclerk (1703–44)   Thomas   Susanna   Catherine
(1700–66) | son of 1st Duke of St Albans
m.1736 | son of Charles II and Nell Gwyn

Topham (1739–80) = Lady Diana Bolingbroke, dau. of 3rd Duke of Marlborough

Charles (1774–1845)
sells Speke 1795

THE WATTS

Watt of Speke

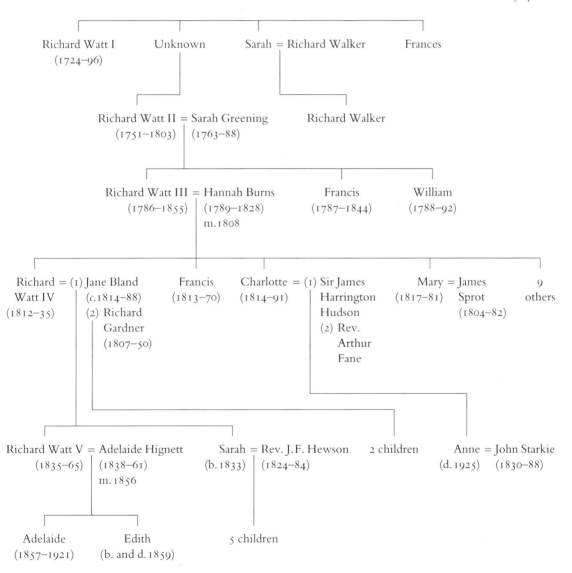

Richard Watt I (1724–96) — Unknown   Sarah = Richard Walker   Frances

Richard Watt II (1751–1803) = Sarah Greening (1763–88)   Richard Walker

Richard Watt III (1786–1855) = Hannah Burns (1789–1828) m.1808   Francis (1787–1844)   William (1788–92)

Richard Watt IV (1812–35) = (1) Jane Bland (c.1814–88) (2) Richard Gardner (1807–50)

Francis (1813–70)

Charlotte (1814–91) = (1) Sir James Harrington Hudson (2) Rev. Arthur Fane

Mary (1817–81) = James Sprot (1804–82)

9 others

Richard Watt V (1835–65) = Adelaide Hignett (1838–61) m.1856

Sarah (b.1833) = Rev. J.F. Hewson (1824–84)

2 children

Anne (d.1925) = John Starkie (1830–88)

Adelaide (1857–1921)   Edith (b. and d.1859)

5 children

BIBLIOGRAPHY

There are Norris Papers in the British Library, Liverpool University Library and the City Record Office, Liverpool City Libraries. Estate Papers for the late nineteenth and early twentieth centuries are also in the City Record Office.

Abstracts from the Norris Papers are printed in J. H. Lumby, 'A Calendar of the Norris Deeds', *Lancashire and Cheshire Record Society*, xciii, 1939, and T. Heywood, 'The Norris Papers', *Chetham Society*, 1846.

ADAMSON, D., and BEAUCLERK-DEWER, P., *The House of Nell Gwyn*, London, 1974.

ANON., 'Speke Hall', *Country Life*, 13, 20 March 1903, pp.336, 368.

DAVEY., P.J., and SPEAKMAN, J., 'Speke Hall: Excavations in the Gardeners' Compound, 1987', *Journal of the Merseyside Archaeological Society*, viii, 1988–9.

DUVAL, M. Susan, 'F. R. Leyland: A Maecenas from Liverpool', *Apollo*, cxxiv, August 1986, pp.110–15.

FARRER, W., and BROWNBILL, J., ed., *Victoria History of the Counties of England: Lancashire*, iii, 1907.

HALL, Samuel Carter, *The Baronial Halls and Ancient Picturesque Edifices of England*, 1858.

HASLAM, Richard, 'Speke Hall Lancashire', *Country Life*, 23 April 1987, pp.98–103.

HIGGINS, D. A., 'Speke Hall: Excavations in the West Range 1981–82', *JMAS*, viii, 1988–9.

HUSSEY, Christopher, 'Speke Hall', *Country Life*, 7, 14 January 1922, pp.16, 48.

LEWIS, Dr J., 'Speke Hall: Archaeology of the East Courtyard, 1989', *JMAS*, viii, 1988–9.

MERRILL, Linda, *The Peacock Room: A Cultural Biography*, 1998.

NICHOLSON, S., 'Farming on a South Lancashire Estate 1066–1795; Evidence from Speke Hall', *JMAS*, iii, 1983.

NORRIS, Edward J., *The Building of Speke Hall*, 1923; rev. ed., 1935.

SAXTON, E. B., 'Speke Hall and Two Norris Inventories, 1624 and 1700', *Transactions of the Historical Society of Lancashire and Cheshire*, xcvi (for 1944), 1945.

SAXTON, E. B., 'A Speke Inventory of 1624', *THSLC*, xcvii (for 1945), 1946.

TAYLOR, Henry, *Old Halls of Lancashire and Cheshire*, 1884, pp.112–17.

TIBBLES, A. J., 'Speke Hall and Frederick Leyland', *Apollo*, May 1994.

WINSTANLEY, H., 'Speke Hall', *THSLC*, lxxix, 1919.

UNPUBLISHED PAPERS

NICHOLSON, Susan, 'Stockton's Wood, Speke, 1981', *The Archaeological Survey of Merseyside*.

TIBBLES, A. J., 'The Gardens at Speke Hall', *Merseyside County Museums*, 1982.

TIBBLES, A. J., 'The Building History of Speke Hall', *Merseyside County Museums*, 1987.